My
First
Book
of
Animals

From A to Z

To Bruce and Juliana
—T. MacC.

Text reviewed by Laurie Roulston, Life Science Educator,
The Museum of Natural History, Denver, CO

Library of Congress Cataloging-in-Publication Data

My first book of animals from A to Z / illustrated by Turi Maccombie.
p.   cm. — (Cartwheel learning bookshelf)
Summary: Illustrations and text depict different kinds of animals from A to Z.
ISBN 0-590-46305-5
1. Animals—Juvenile literature.   2. English language—Alphabet—Juvenile literature.
[1. Animals.   2. Alphabet.]   I. Maccombie, Turi, ill.   II. Scholastic Inc.   III. Series.
QL49.M9   1994   591—dc20   [E]   92-19284   CIP   AC

12   11   10   9   8   7   6   5   4   3   2   1   4   5   6   7   8/9
Printed in Singapore

First Scholastic printing, March 1994

My First Book
of Animals

From A to Z

More Than 150 Animals
Every Child Should Know

by Christopher Egan, Lorraine Hopping Egan,
Thomas Campbell Jackson, and Diane Molleson

Illustrated by Turi MacCombie

Cartwheel
·B·O·O·K·S·™

SCHOLASTIC INC.
New York Toronto London Auckland Sydney

A

Aardvark

Classification: Mammal
Home: Africa, between Ethiopia and the Cape of Good Hope
Adult Size: 4–6 feet long; 60–140 pounds
Food: Ants and termites

Aardvarks have sticky tongues that can be 18 inches long! Aardvarks use their tongues to catch ants and termites.

Aardvark mothers usually have only one baby at a time. Babies are born in the late spring and early summer. Mother aardvarks teach their babies how to use their sharp claws to rip open ant and termite nests in the ground. At the age of two, a young aardvark goes out on its own.

Alligator

Classification: Reptile
Home: Southeastern United States (especially Florida) and the Yangtze River basin of China
Adult Size: 5–15 feet long; 100–550 pounds
Food: Fish, frogs and other water animals, birds and small mammals

During the day, alligators sun themselves on riverbanks or float underwater. Just before nightfall, they hunt by grunting and slapping the water. Scared fish scatter. Many of them rush right into the alligators' open jaws!

Mother alligators lay about 25 eggs each summer. Many of the hatchlings are eaten by bigger animals. The mother protects as many babies as she can. At about five or six years old, alligators are adults. Then their only enemies are humans.

Armadillo

Classification: Mammal
Home: Warm climates in North and South America from Texas to Argentina
Adult Size: 5–60 inches long; less than 1 pound to 20 pounds
Food: Insects, millipedes, worms, termites, ants, and other small animals

An armadillo has a "suit of armor" made of bony plates. When an armadillo is attacked by a coyote or another enemy, it curls into a ball. The plates protect its soft underside.

An armadillo mother usually has about four babies at a time, but she can have as many as twelve. The babies will be either all male or all female, because armadillos never have mixed litters.

B

Baboon

Classification: Mammal
Home: Africa and Saudi Arabia
Adult Size: 25–45 inches tall; 30–100 pounds
Food: Fruits, grains, grass, flowers, nuts, leaves, eggs, insects, hares, and other small animals

Baboons live in troops that can have between 10 and 300 members. There are often twice as many female baboons as there are males. There are always more young baboons than grown-ups. Male baboons are bigger than females. Males protect the troop from enemies.

Baboon mothers have one baby at a time. Baboon infants cling to their mothers with their hands and feet. They cannot take care of themselves. Their mothers will teach them how to hunt.

Bat

Classification: Mammal
Home: Everywhere but Antarctica
Adult Size: 2–15 inches long; less than 1 ounce to 2 pounds
Food: Fruit, insects, and the blood of other animals

Bats are the only mammals that fly. They leave their caves to hunt at dusk. Bats can't see very well, so to get around they squeak. The squeaks bounce off objects and return to the bats' big ears. If the echoes return quickly, that means the object is close—and large!

Bat mothers do not raise their young in nests. For the first few weeks a baby bat hangs on tightly to its mother as she flies around. When the baby is older, the mother bat will leave it at home in the cave while she goes out looking for food.

Bear

Classification: Mammal
Home: Cooler climates of North America, Europe, Asia, and the Arctic
Adult Size: 3–11 feet tall; 60–1,600 pounds
Food: Insects, fish, seals and sea lions, small land mammals, fruits, honey, and other vegetation

Bears can't see well, but they can smell food miles away. All spring, summer, and fall, bears eat as much as they can to fatten up for winter.

Bears spend the winter in dens. But, they are *not* hibernating. They are just in a deep sleep! Sometimes they come out of their dens, but only on warm winter days.

Mother bears have their babies during the winter sleep period. The cubs stay in the den until springtime. Then they come outside, ready to play.

Beaver

Classification: Mammal
Home: Rivers, streams, and lakes in North America and Northern Europe
Adult Size: 4–5 feet long; 40 pounds
Food: Bark, tree shoots, leaves, herbs, grass, and other vegetation

Using its 20 teeth and two front paws, a beaver can build a giant dam from trees. The beaver lives in and around the pools of water created by the dam. Beavers build lodges and store food for the winter. A beaver uses its large, webbed feet for swimming and its broad, flat tail as a paddle. If an enemy comes too near, a beaver will beat its tail on the ground to warn other beavers!

Baby beavers are called kits. They live in the beaver lodge with their parents until they are two years old. Then they have to leave to make room for new babies.

7

BIRDS

Birds are warm-blooded animals. Every bird has two wings, a backbone, a beak, and feathers.

Bluejay

Cardinal

Owl

Finch

Ostrich

Hawk

Robin

Parakeet

Flamingo

Hummingbird

Chicken

Swan

C

Camel

Classification: Mammal
Home: Desert regions of central Asia, the Near East, northern Africa, and Australia
Adult Size: 70–90 inches high; 550–1400 pounds
Food: Desert plants

The camel can live for days without water. Its big, tough lips help the camel chew thorny plants. In a desert sandstorm, its long eyelashes protect the camel's eyes.

A camel is ideal for life in the desert. This "ship of the desert" may have one or two humps. During long journeys, fat stored in the camel's hump turns into food energy.

Mother camels have one baby each year. A baby camel is called a foal. It can run just hours after birth. The camel calls to its mother with a soft *baa* that sounds a lot like a lamb.

Canary

Canary

Classification: Bird
Home: The Canary Islands, Madeira, and the Azores Islands
Adult Size: 4–5 inches long; about half an ounce
Food: Seeds

Canaries are a type of finch. Humans keep tame canaries as pets. People like to listen to the pretty songs that the male canary sings. Tame canaries are yellow, but wild canaries are usually dark green.

Wild canaries build nests high off the ground. A female canary lays four or five eggs in the nest. When the babies are born, the mother feeds them and teaches them to fly. Once they can fly, the canaries are ready to leave the nest and raise families of their own.

Cat

Classification: Mammal
Home: All the continents but Antarctica
Adult Size: 8–12 inches high; 6–20 pounds
Food: Fish, chicken, beef, seafood, mice, birds, snakes, and other small animals.

Tamed cats have lived in human homes for thousands of years. They are much smaller than big cats such as lions and tigers. But they have the same basic tools for hunting—long canine teeth, padded paws for sneaking up on prey, and sharp claws for tearing.

There are three to eight kittens in a mother cat's litter. They are born blind and helpless. Within two weeks, their eyes open and they can see. Their mother teaches them to hunt. They like to practice hunting by stalking and pouncing on string and cat toys, even though humans may feed them ready-made cat food all of their lives!

Cheetah

Classification: Mammal
Home: The plains of northern Africa, the Middle East, and India
Adult Size: About 3 feet high; 110–140 pounds
Food: Antelopes, rodents, hares, birds, and other animals

Cheetahs are cats. Most cats hunt at night. But cheetahs hunt in the early morning light because they are the only big cats that can run faster than their prey. They sprint at 55 miles per hour. They do not need to hunt under the cover of night.

Cheetah mothers have litters of one to eight cubs. The cubs are born with their eyes closed. Newborn cheetahs have long, gray fur. At three months, the cubs grow new coats with dark fur spots.

Chimpanzee

Classification: Mammal
Home: Forests in Africa
Adult Size: 50–65 inches high; 90–110 pounds
Food: Fruits and other vegetation

Chimpanzees are apes. They live in family groups in the forest. The families are made up of one male, several females, and their babies. At night, the family builds a nest of leafy branches in a tree for sleeping. During the day, they eat, play, and groom each others' fur.

At first, a baby chimp will ride under its mother's body, gripping her chest and being supported by her arm. At five months old, the baby will ride on her back. The young chimp will stay with its mother until the age of six.

11

Cow (Cattle)

Classification: Mammal
Home: All the continents but Antarctica
Adult Size: 5–7 feet; 900–2,000 pounds
Food: Grass and other vegetation

A herd of cattle is made up of male bulls, female heifers, and cows. A heifer becomes a cow after her first calf is born.

Some wild cattle live in Asia. But domesticated cattle live almost everywhere humans do. Some people use big, strong cattle called oxen for plowing and other heavy jobs. Humans also raise cattle for beef and milk.

Cows usually have one calf per year. The calf will drink its mother's milk for about ten months.

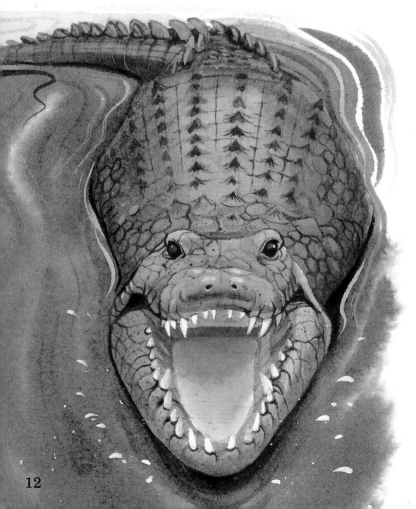

Crocodile

Classification: Reptile
Home: Rivers, lakes, coastal waters in northern Africa, Australia, Southeast Asia, and the southern United States
Adult Size: 4–23 feet long; 66–360 pounds
Food: Fish and turtles

Crocodiles have large, strong jaws and long teeth. Unlike the alligator, the crocodile's snout comes to a point. When a crocodile hunts, it crawls slowly and quietly, then pounces on its victim. Sometimes the crocodile floats very still. If an animal wanders near, the crocodile swallows it whole!

A mother crocodile can lay up to 50 eggs. She stays near her nest to protect them. When the unborn crocodile begins to grunt from inside its egg, it is ready to hatch. The baby has a special egg tooth for breaking its shell.

D

Deer

Classification: Mammal
Home: North and South America, Europe, Asia, and northwest Africa
Adult Size: 1–7 feet high at the shoulder; 20–200 pounds
Food: Grass, leaves, flowers, and other vegetation

Deer are cud chewers. Like all cud chewers, they swallow lots of food and store it in their stomachs. Later, they bring up the stored food, and chew it until they can easily digest it.

Baby deer are called fawns. Most fawns are born with white spots on their coats. Within a year, the fawns will lose their spots. The male deer, called bucks, grow antlers.

Desert Animals

Oryx

Camel

Desert Hedgehog

Scorpion

Kangaroo Rat

Fennic Fox

14

North American Desert

Elf Owl

Puma

Kit Fox

Roadrunner

Gila Monster

Rattlesnake

Jackrabbit

15

Dog

Classification: Mammal
Home: All over the world
Adult Size: 5–35 inches high at the shoulder;
   $1\frac{1}{2}$–200 pounds
Food: Chicken, beef, fish, eggs, cheese, and small animals

Dogs come in many breeds. Some dogs are mixed breeds. Dogs that are all one breed are called purebreds. The smallest breed, the chihuahua, stands only five inches high at its shoulder. The biggest, the Irish wolfhound, is almost three feet tall.

Baby dogs are called puppies. Puppies are born with their eyes closed and their ears sealed. About fifteen days after birth, their ears and eyes open. The best time to adopt a puppy is when it is six to eight weeks old.

16

Dolphin

Classification: Mammal
Home: Warm, shallow water throughout the Atlantic and Pacific oceans, the North and Mediterranean seas, Southeast Asia, and South America
Adult Size: 3–30 feet long; 100 pounds to 9 tons
Food: Squid, fish, and shrimp

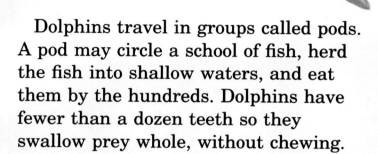

Dolphins travel in groups called pods. A pod may circle a school of fish, herd the fish into shallow waters, and eat them by the hundreds. Dolphins have fewer than a dozen teeth so they swallow prey whole, without chewing.

Female dolphins have one calf at a time. The baby dolphin lives with its mother until it is three years old.

Duck

Classification: Bird
Home: Lakes and ponds on all the continents but Antarctica
Adult Size: 1–2 feet long; 1–16 pounds
Food: Plants, grass, roots, seeds, insects, snails, barnacles, shrimp, and mussels

Ducks can fly, swim, and walk. Their webbed feet are like paddles in water. Their waterproof feathers keep them warm and dry.

Males are usually more brightly colored than females. Females build nests on land. They lay four to 12 eggs in the nest. When the ducklings hatch, they stay with their mothers for about nine weeks, when they can fly. The mothers teach the ducklings to fly by taking to the air and then calling for the young to follow.

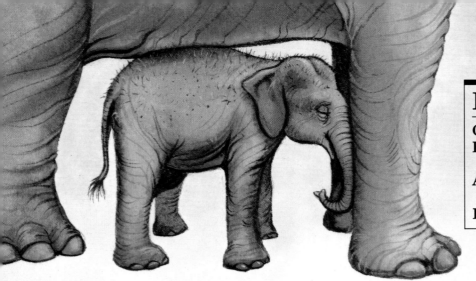

E

Elephant

Classification: Mammal
Home: Grasslands of central Africa, India, and Southeast Asia
Adult Size: 8–11 feet high at the shoulder; 4–6 tons
Food: Grass and other vegetation

An elephant's nose is a long trunk, strong enough to lift logs and precise enough to pick up a lump of sugar. The elephant uses its tusks to dig for food or fight an enemy. Its big ears are not just for hearing. When the elephant is threatened, it can fan out its ears so that it looks even bigger!

Elephant mothers carry their babies for 22 months before giving birth. Most give birth to only one baby at a time, but sometimes they have twins. A baby elephant will live with its mother until it is about 14 years old.

Elk

Classification: Mammal
Home: Mountains, woodlands, bogs, and marshes in western North America and parts of Europe
Adult Size: 3–5 feet high at the shoulder; 450–800 pounds
Food: Shoots, twigs and bark of sapling trees, grass, and other vegetation

Elk are a very vocal type of deer. When they are threatened, young elk squeal, adult males bark, and mothers neigh to their young. All that noise helps to scare away their main enemy, the cougar.

Elk mothers are called cows. They give birth each May or June. A cow can have one or two calves at a time. The calves are born light brown with white spots. The spots disappear by August. By age three, the elk are ready to become parents themselves.

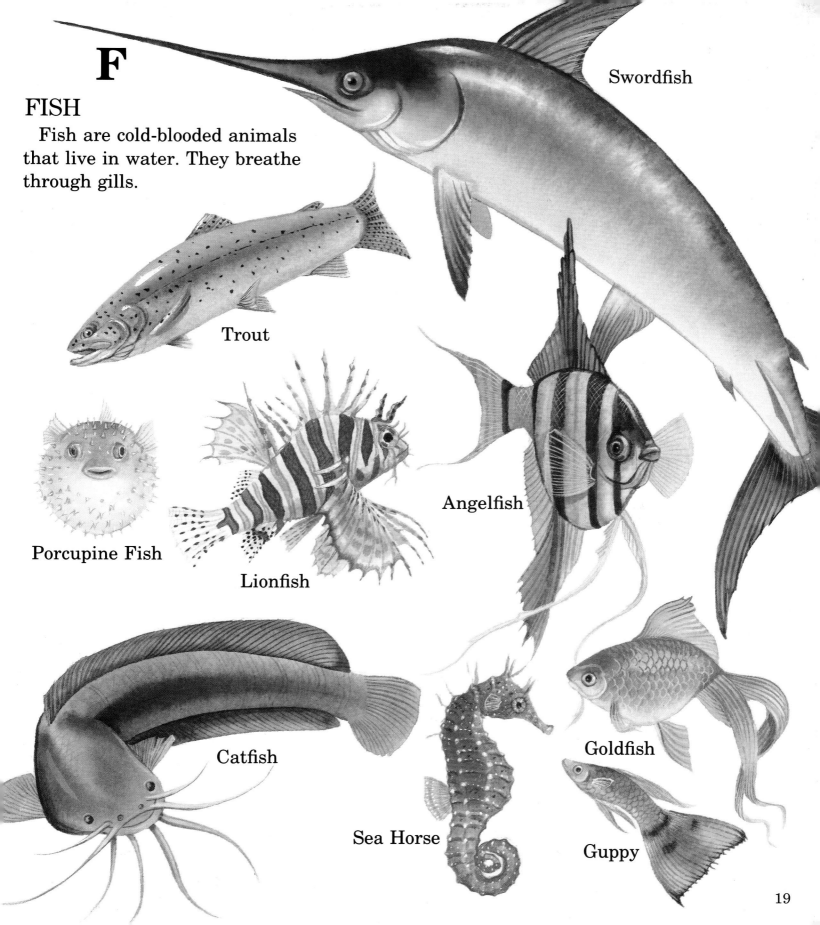

F

FISH

Fish are cold-blooded animals that live in water. They breathe through gills.

Swordfish

Trout

Porcupine Fish

Lionfish

Angelfish

Catfish

Sea Horse

Goldfish

Guppy

19

Fox

Classification: Mammal
Home: North America, Europe, northern Asia, the Arctic, northern South America, North Africa, and Sudan
Adult Size: $2-4\frac{1}{2}$ feet long; 2–15 pounds
Food: Birds, rabbits, moles, mice, voles, fish, lemmings, eggs, grass, fruits, and other vegetation

With their long bodies, short legs, and pointy snouts, foxes look a lot like dogs and wolves. Their coats come in many colors—white, red, brown, and more. Their tall ears pick up the slightest sound of moving prey.

Fox families live in burrows. A family includes a mother and three to eight cubs. The newborn foxes are born blind, but they open their eyes after eight or nine days. Their thick fur keeps them warm.

Frog

Classification: Amphibian
Home: Warm water regions on all continents except Antarctica
Adult Size: Less than 1 inch to 10 inches long; less than 1 pound
Food: Earthworms, snails, insects, spiders, fish, birds, and mice

Frogs have wet skin and live on land and in the water. Their strong hind legs help them jump and swim. Their bulging eyes help them quickly spot moving insects. Frogs flick their sticky tongues to catch their prey.

Baby frogs are called tadpoles. They have tails but no legs. Tadpoles live in the water and breathe through gills. As they grow older, tadpoles lose their gills and tails and grow four legs. They develop lungs to breathe air while they are on land.

Gazelle

Classification: Mammal
Home: Plains and mountains in western and central Asia, India, and northern and eastern Africa
Adult Size: 25–30 inches high at the shoulder; 25–185 pounds
Food: Twigs, bark, and grass

Gazelles are a type of antelope. Most kinds have round, black horns shaped like the letter V. All gazelles have long legs and can run faster than their enemies—except for the cheetah. Most gazelles can go for long periods without drinking much water. They can get by on droplets of dew.

Gazelles live together in small herds. A female gives birth to one baby at a time, although some twins are born.

Giraffe

Classification: Mammal
Home: Grasslands of Africa, south of the Sahara Desert
Adult Size: 15–18 feet high; 1,000–3,000 pounds
Food: Acacia leaves, climbing plants, and other vegetation

Since they are the tallest creatures on Earth, giraffes have a food supply all to themselves—leaves two stories off the ground! The giraffe's dark tongue can stick out nearly two feet to safely eat leaves surrounded by sharp thorns.

A mother giraffe gives birth to one calf at a time. When they are born, baby giraffes are about six feet tall—that's taller than most humans! The newborns weigh about 150 pounds at birth. Young giraffes drink milk from their mothers while they learn to eat leaves from the trees.

21

Goat

Classification: Mammal
Home: Farms and wild mountain areas
around the world, except Antarctica
Adult Size: 2–7 feet high; 40–500 pounds
Food: Bushes, leaves, tree bark, grass shrubs, corn,
oats, cereal, grains, and hay

For at least 9,000 years, humans have raised goats for warm wool and creamy milk. More people in the world drink goats' milk than cows' milk. In the wild, goats live in mountain areas and are excellent climbers and jumpers.

Adult males are called bucks or billy goats. Adult females are called does or nanny goats. Baby goats are called kids.

Gorilla

Classification: Mammal
Home: Rainforests of Africa
Adult Size: 6 feet tall; 200–450 pounds
Food: Tree bark, flowers, leaves, fruit, and insects

Gorillas are like humans in many ways. Gorillas travel in troops, which are a lot like families. Every night the troop builds simple nests in or near a tree. Adult gorillas build their own nests. Baby gorillas sleep with their mothers. Gorillas never sleep in the same nest twice.

Gorilla mothers carry their babies piggyback until they are three months old. That's when the babies learn to crawl. But even after they can walk, gorilla babies spend much of their first three years riding piggyback on their mothers. At eight years old, the young gorillas are ready to be mothers and fathers themselves.

Hamster

Classification: Mammal
Home: Asia, Europe
Adult Size: 7–11 inches long; 4–32 ounces
Food: Fruits, seeds, green vegetation, and some small animals

Hamsters are small, furry rodents with large cheek pouches. These pouches are useful for carrying food to the hamsters' nests. Hamsters collect food and store it in piles, one type of food to a pile. Then in winter, when food is scarce outside the nest, hamsters can live off the stored food.

Wild hamsters usually have two litters per year. Pet hamsters have more. Each litter has about six or seven babies.

Hippopotamus

Classification: Mammal
Home: Rivers and other wet areas of Africa south of the Sahara Desert
Adult Size: 4–5 $\frac{1}{2}$ feet high at the shoulder; 400 pounds to 3 $\frac{1}{2}$ tons
Food: Grass and fallen fruits

On land, the hippo's short, stubby legs can barely hold it up. The skin and fat alone weigh half a ton! So it is no wonder that the heavy hippo spends most of its time in water. The blue-gray skin matches the color of the water, keeping the animals hidden from lions and other predators.

A newborn hippo weighs about 100 pounds. It can swim almost immediately. As its mother rests in the water, a young hippo will often climb on her back to sunbathe!

Honeybee

Classification: Insect
Home: Just about everywhere except polar regions
Adult Size: Up to 1 inch long; far less than 1 ounce
Food: Flower pollen and nectar

Between 50 and 60 thousand honeybees live together in one hive. A group of honeybees is called a colony. The most important insect in the colony is the queen bee. She lays a thousand or more eggs each day of summer.

In the hive, there are only a few hundred males. They are called drones. There are thousands of female workers. Their job is to guard the nest and bring back food—nectar and pollen from flowers. The bees eat the pollen and turn the nectar into honey, which they store in wax honeycombs.

Horse

Classification: Mammal
Home: All over the world, except for polar regions
Adult Size: 4–5½ feet high at the shoulder; 500–2,200 pounds
Food: Grass, hay, apples, and other vegetation

Wild horses live in herds led by a male horse called a stallion. Females are called mares, and usually have one foal (or baby) each spring. The foal learns to stand and run in its first few hours of life.

Some horses, such as mustangs, live in the wild. But most are bred by humans for riding, racing, showing, and working.

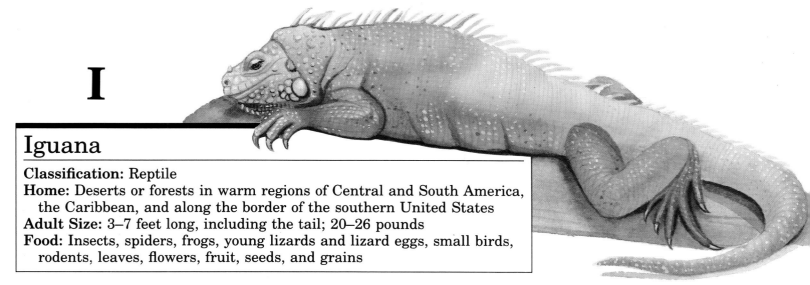

I

Iguana

Classification: Reptile
Home: Deserts or forests in warm regions of Central and South America, the Caribbean, and along the border of the southern United States
Adult Size: 3–7 feet long, including the tail; 20–26 pounds
Food: Insects, spiders, frogs, young lizards and lizard eggs, small birds, rodents, leaves, flowers, fruit, seeds, and grains

Iguanas have tails that can be twice as long as their bodies. These sun-loving lizards warm their bodies all morning and eat in the afternoon. Some young iguanas eat more meat than their parents!

A mother iguana may travel up to two miles to find a safe nest site. When she finds one, she digs a tunnel where she lays up to 30 eggs and buries them for safety. Two months later, the young hatch and dig their way to the surface.

Impala

Classification: Mammal
Home: Grasslands in Africa from Kenya to South Africa
Adult Size: $2\frac{1}{2}$–3 feet high at the shoulder; 100–180 pounds
Food: Grass, leaves, and other vegetation

The impala is a beautiful red-orange gazelle. It can leap 30 feet in a single bound—more than two car-lengths—and ten feet high! The graceful animal jumps, runs, and hops in a zigzag pattern to escape lions, cheetahs, and other predators. A sharp, loud bark warns other impalas of danger.

At first the newborn is alone with its mother. When the pair rejoins the herd, the fawns spend more time with each other than with their mothers!

INSECTS

Insects are small animals whose bodies are divided into three parts. They have six legs and usually two pairs of wings.

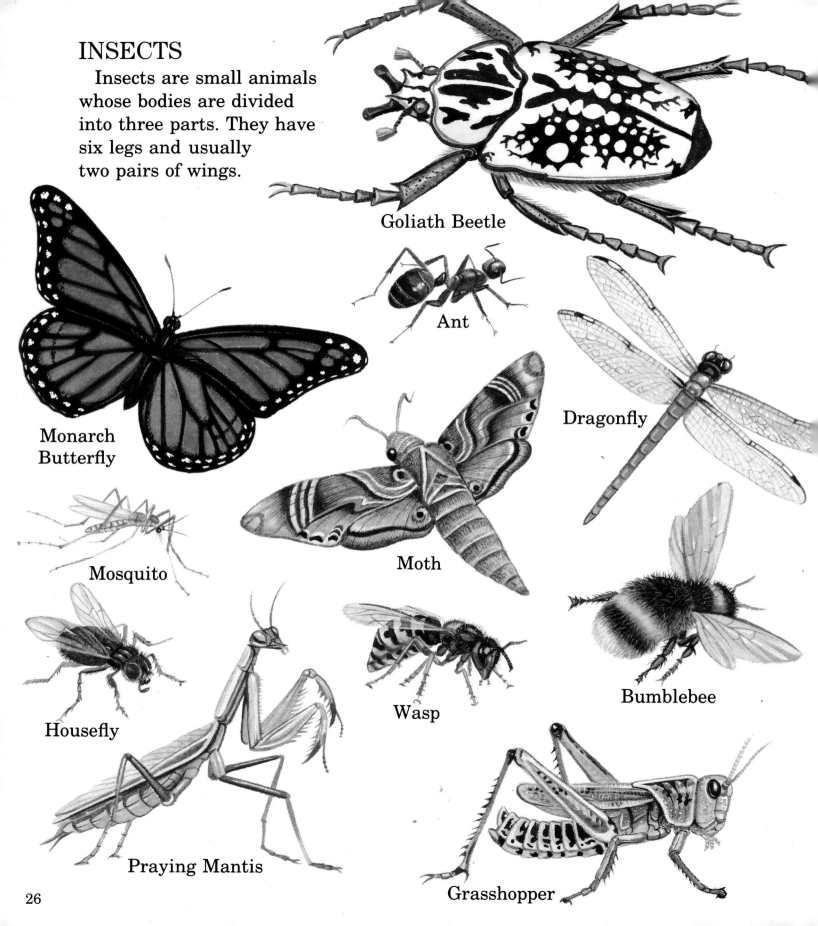

Goliath Beetle

Monarch Butterfly

Ant

Dragonfly

Moth

Mosquito

Housefly

Praying Mantis

Wasp

Bumblebee

Grasshopper

J

Jaguar

Classification: Mammal
Home: Tropical forests and marshes in Central and South America
Adult Size: 15–30 inches high; 150–400 pounds
Food: Horses, birds, tortoises, fish, caimans, monkeys, and other animals

Jaguars are the fiercest animals in Central and South America. They will even attack caimans, who are in the same family as crocodiles! Jaguars are nocturnal. That means they hunt at night and sleep during the day. Their dark spots keep them well hidden.

Baby jaguars are helpless. When they are very young, they nurse from their mothers. They live with their mothers for two years, while learning to hunt. When a female jaguar is about three, she is old enough to become a mother herself.

Jellyfish

Classification: Jellyfish
Home: All oceans, both deep and coastal waters
Adult Size: Microscopic to 7 feet
Food: Fish and other sea animals

A jellyfish is not a fish. It is a sea animal called a medusa. It has no bones, so its body is squishy like jelly. The jellyfish is very lightweight. That helps it float in water. The tides and ocean currents carry jellyfish from place to place.

Jellyfish hatch from eggs. The baby jellyfish attach themselves to the ocean floor. When they are big enough, they break away. They grow to full size as they float in the ocean.

Kangaroo

Classification: Mammal
Home: Australia, Tasmania, and New Guinea
Adult Size: 3–7 feet; 50–150 pounds
Food: Grass and other vegetation

K

Kangaroos sometimes live alone, but when food and water are scarce, they get together in groups called mobs to search for grassy areas.

Kangaroos are the world's largest marsupials—animals that grow up in a mother's pouch. A newborn starts out the size of a thumb! It is blind and hairless. The baby kangaroo, called a joey, grows very fast and soon begins jumping out of the pouch from time to time. After about eight months, the young kangaroo leaves the pouch for good, ready to hop on its own big, strong hind legs.

Koala

Classification: Mammal
Home: Eucalyptus trees in Australia
Adult Size: 2–3 feet high; 10–35 pounds
Food: Eucalyptus leaves

Koalas may look like teddy bears, but they are not bears at all! Like kangaroos, they are marsupials. When the young koala is six months old, it leaves its mother's pouch and clings tightly to her back or shoulders until it is nearly full-grown.

Koalas eat only leaves and young shoots from eucalyptus trees. They spend most of their time in trees. The only time they touch the ground is when they switch to another tree.

Ladybug (or Ladybird Beetle)

Classification: Insect
Home: Widespread throughout North America
Adult Size: $\frac{1}{10} - \frac{3}{10}$ of an inch; less than .0035 ounces
Food: Aphids, plant lice, other insects, and small animals

Ladybugs are small beetles. Ladybugs can be males or females, despite their name.

These tiny hunters are welcome on farms and in gardens because they eat many insects that destroy crops.

Ladybugs hatch from eggs. At first, their wings and bodies are a yellowish color. As they get older, they turn red with black spots.

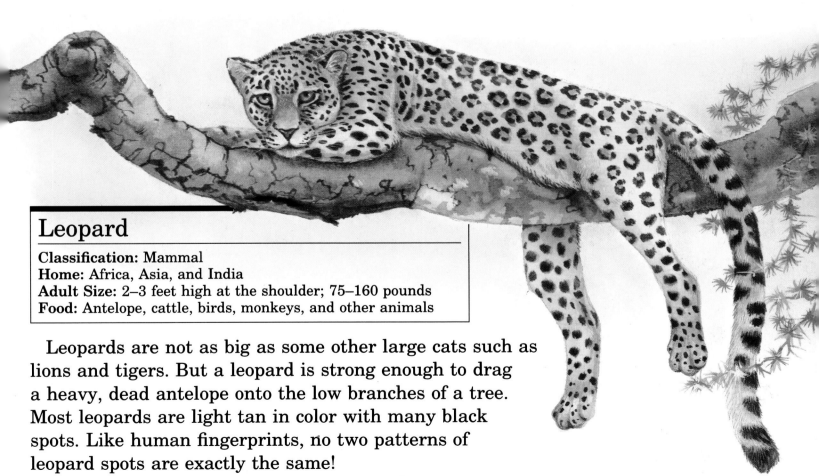

Leopard

Classification: Mammal
Home: Africa, Asia, and India
Adult Size: 2–3 feet high at the shoulder; 75–160 pounds
Food: Antelope, cattle, birds, monkeys, and other animals

Leopards are not as big as some other large cats such as lions and tigers. But a leopard is strong enough to drag a heavy, dead antelope onto the low branches of a tree. Most leopards are light tan in color with many black spots. Like human fingerprints, no two patterns of leopard spots are exactly the same!

Baby leopards are born with their eyes shut. Mother leopards protect their babies and teach them how to hunt.

Lion

Classification: Mammal
Home: Africa (south of the Sahara) and India
Adult Size: 8–9 feet long; 250–400 pounds
Food: Large prey—antelopes, giraffes, zebras, and other meat

Lions travel in groups called prides. The pride is usually made up of one to five males, up to 15 lionesses, and the cubs. Each pride stakes out its own territory. The pride will hunt animals and drink water only in its own territory.

Wild lionesses usually give birth to two or three cubs at a time. Lion cubs nurse from their mother for six or seven months. When it is time for them to eat meat, she coaxes them over to an animal she has killed.

Then the mother teaches the young lions to catch their own meals. When male lion cubs are two or three years old, they are ready to fend for themselves.

Lobster

Classification: Crustacean
Home: European waters and coastal waters of the northern Atlantic and Pacific oceans
Adult Size: 7–37 inches long; 1–20 pounds
Food: Crabs, snails, small fish, and other lobsters

Lobsters have five sets of legs. Their front legs are called claws. One claw is always bigger than the other. Lobsters use their claws to grab and tear food.

A mother lobster lays thousands of eggs at a time. She carries them under her tail for a year. The babies rise to the surface and drift for about two months. Many are easy prey for fish and birds. The few survivors sink to the ocean bottom and grow into adults.

M

Manatee

Classification: Mammal
Home: Coastal waters near Florida, the Caribbean, South America; river basins in Brazil and West Africa
Adult Size: 6–15 feet long; 1,000–3,500 pounds
Food: Seagrass and other water plants

Manatees are huge, slow-moving sea mammals. Their front legs are shaped like paddles for steering. Manatees must come to the surface to breathe every 12 to 15 minutes.

A mother manatee gives birth to a calf once every three to five years. The mother shows the calf where to find food and how to get to warm waters in winter. In murky water the mother and calf will find each other by calling and listening.

Monkey

Classification: Mammal
Home: Tropical areas of Africa, Asia, and Central and South America
Adult Size: 6–32 inches, not including tail; 3–150 pounds
Food: Fruit, leaves, and eggs

There are many different kinds of monkeys. They are excellent climbers and spend most of their time in trees. Troops of monkeys run along high branches looking for food. They spend many hours picking dirt and bugs from one another's hair.

Baby monkeys are usually born one at a time. At first a baby stays close to its mother. When the baby is older, it rides around on her back until it is ready to walk and climb alone.

31

Mountain Animals

Snow Leopard

Golden Eagle

Vicuña

Yak

Pika

Mountain Goat

Bighorn Sheep

Mountain Lion

Giant Panda

33

Moose

Classification: Mammal
Home: Forests, swamps, and thickets in North America, from northern Canada to Colorado and Maine
Adult Size: 6–7½ feet high at the shoulder; 700–1,400 pounds
Food: Twigs, bark, flower buds, water lilies, and other vegetation

The moose is the largest deer in the world. All spring and summer, the male grows big, full antlers for fighting. He sheds them in winter.

Females give birth to one or two calves at a time. The calves learn to walk and swim in just two weeks!

Mouse

Classification: Mammal
Home: Fields, woods, and most other habitats everywhere except Antarctica
Adult Size: 5–16 inches (including the tail); less than 1 ounce to 3 ounces
Food: Seeds, grains, fruits, nuts, and other vegetation; insects, caterpillars, spiders, and other small animals

Most people know the common house mouse, but there are hundreds of kinds of mice. All mice have two front teeth. They use them to gnaw at their food. A mouse's front teeth will grow for its entire life.

Newborn mice have pink skin and no fur. Their fur doesn't grow in until they are 10 days old. At 45 days, a female mouse is old enough to have her own litter.

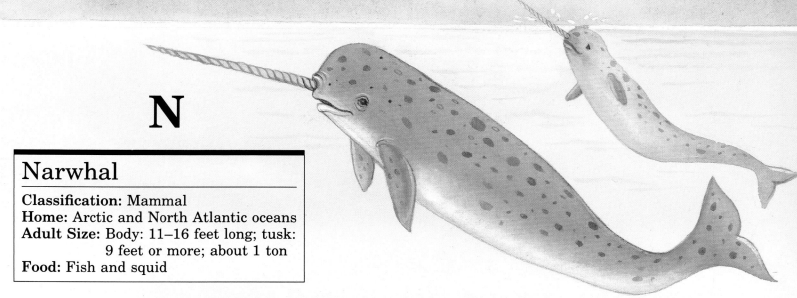

N

Narwhal

Classification: Mammal
Home: Arctic and North Atlantic oceans
Adult Size: Body: 11–16 feet long; tusk:
    9 feet or more; about 1 ton
Food: Fish and squid

Narwhals are small whales. They live in cold northern oceans. A male narwhal has a tusk that is really an overgrown tooth. The narwhal has no other teeth.

As soon as a calf is born, a mother narwhal pushes it to the surface for its first breath. The calf drinks its mother's milk for six months. Then it can start to catch fish for itself.

Newt

Classification: Amphibian
Home: Throughout the Northern Hemisphere
Adult Size: 3–7 inches long; ½ ounce
Food: Insects, snails, and worms

Newts are salamanders. They live in damp woods or around ponds. Some newts have poisonous skins.

Newt eggs hatch into larvae. The larvae have gills for breathing. Adult newts lose their gills and breathe air. Some newts live in water all their lives. Others move to land as adults.

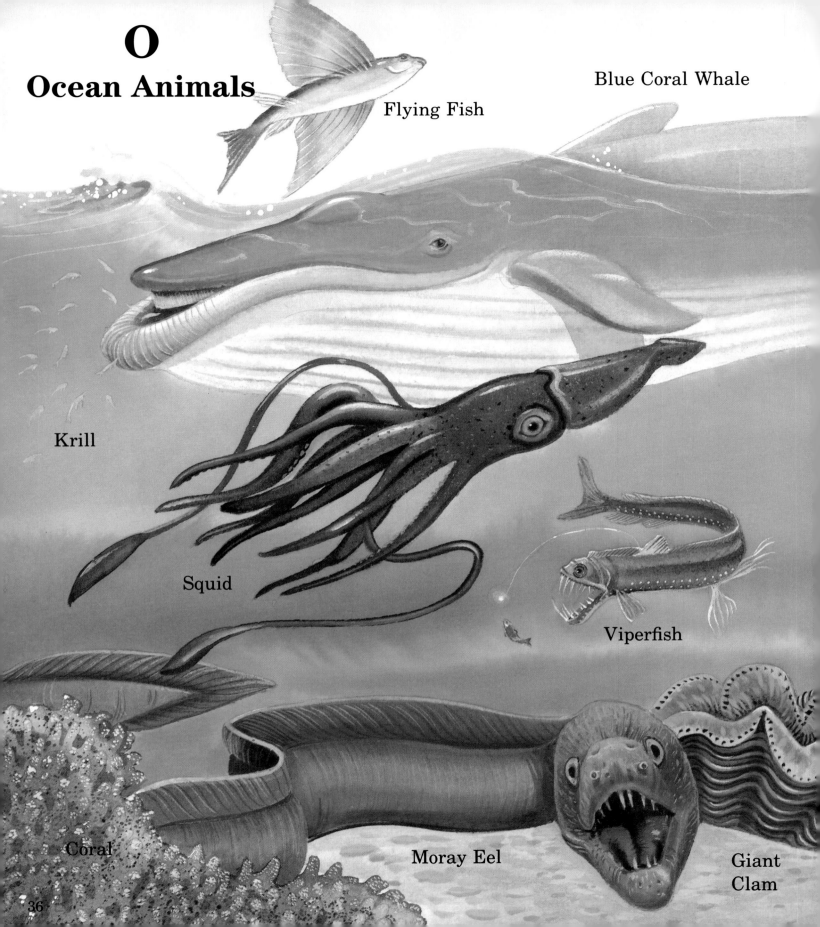

O
Ocean Animals

Flying Fish

Blue Coral Whale

Krill

Squid

Viperfish

Coral

Moray Eel

Giant Clam

36

Jellyfish

Ray

Tuna

Grouper

Sea Snake

Flounder

Starfish

37

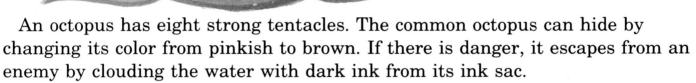

Octopus

Classification: Mollusk
Home: Atlantic, Pacific, and Indian oceans, and the Mediterranean Sea
Adult Size: Varies by species, from 2 inches to over 25 feet; 1 ounce to 100 pounds
Food: Crabs, lobsters, and shellfish

An octopus has eight strong tentacles. The common octopus can hide by changing its color from pinkish to brown. If there is danger, it escapes from an enemy by clouding the water with dark ink from its ink sac.

A mother octopus lays thousands of eggs. The eggs attach to rocks on the ocean floor. The mother guards her eggs for about six weeks until they hatch. The young octopuses then swim near the surface, where many get eaten by other animals.

Opossum

Classification: Mammal
Home: North, Central, and South America
Adult Size: 25–40 inches, including tail; up to 13 pounds
Food: Fruit, plants, berries, mushrooms, eggs, insects, and snakes

The opossum sleeps in hollow trees during the day. It looks for food at night. When it is in danger, the opossum lies perfectly still and pretends to be dead. This is called "playin' 'possum."

Mother opossums have about a dozen tiny babies. The babies crawl into their mother's pouch and drink her milk for about eight weeks. When the babies grow too big for the pouch, they ride around on their mother's back.

Orangutan

Classification: Mammal
Home: Southeast Asia
Adult Size: 3–5 feet tall, 80–200 pounds
Food: Fruit and leaves

Orangutans are apes. They live in trees and swing from branch to branch by their strong arms. An orangutan hardly ever comes down to the ground. Every night it sleeps in a new nest it builds in the branches.

A four-pound newborn orangutan needs a lot of care. It holds on to its mother's hair as she moves from tree to tree. A baby stays with its mother for about four years.

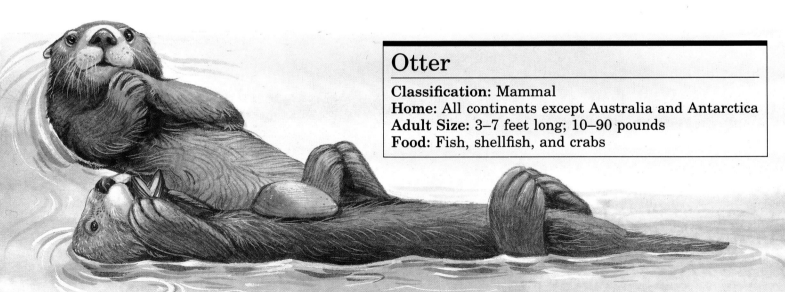

Otter

Classification: Mammal
Home: All continents except Australia and Antarctica
Adult Size: 3–7 feet long; 10–90 pounds
Food: Fish, shellfish, and crabs

Many otters live near rivers or lakes. They like to slide down muddy banks. Sea otters float on their backs in beds of ocean seaweed. They use rocks to crack open their food.

Newborn otter pups need their mothers for everything. At first the pups can't swim or even see. An otter pup stays with its mother for a year, drinking her milk and learning how to dive for food.

Panda

Classification: Mammal
Home: Mountains of Southwestern China, Tibet, and Nepal
Adult Size: 3–6 feet long; up to 300 pounds
Food: Bamboo shoots, roots, honey, and grass

The giant panda is a rare animal. It looks like a black-and-white bear. But it is really in a family all its own. Giant pandas spend most of their time eating bamboo.

A panda cub weighs just a quarter of a pound at birth. Its mother carries the tiny baby around with her everywhere. The babies don't open their eyes for 40 days. A panda cub stays with its mother until it is one and a half years old.

Peacock

Classification: Bird
Home: India, Sri Lanka
Adult Size: Males 6–8 feet long, including four feet of tail feathers; up to 11 pounds
Food: Plants, berries, insects, and frogs

A male peacock has beautiful blue and green feathers. His long tail feathers have big spots that look like eyes. The male peacock shows off his colorful feathers to attract a female.

A mother peacock lays several eggs. They hatch after a month. She has no fancy feathers. Colorful feathers would help hungry animals find her nest and her young ones.

Penguin

Classification: Bird
Home: Southern Hemisphere, especially Antarctica
Adult Size: 1–4 feet tall, 3–90 pounds
Food: Fish, squid, shrimp, and krill

Penguins are birds that can't fly. But they are excellent swimmers. They use their short wings as paddles. They steer with their webbed feet. Thick waterproof feathers keep them warm and dry. Penguins are very sociable and gather in huge colonies.

Mother and father take turns feeding the fuzzy, gray penguin chicks. The chicks cannot go into the water until they have grown their black and white feathers.

Pig

Classification: Mammal
Home: All continents except Antarctica
Adult Size: 2–6 feet long; up to 600 pounds
Food: Almost anything, especially corn and alfalfa

Pigs are smart! They have good reasons for rolling around in the mud. It keeps them cool and protects them from insects.

Mothers have six to twelve piglets in a litter. Each piglet weighs two or three pounds. Each piglet always nurses from the same spot.

Plains Animals
African Plains

African Elephant

Giraffe

Gazelle

Cheetah

Hyena

Lion

Leopard

42

American Plains

Coyote

Plains
Pocket Gopher

Ground Squirrel

Prairie Dog

Jackrabbit

Badger

43

Platypus

Classification: Mammal
Home: Australia, Tasmania
Adult Size: Up to 2 feet long; about 4 pounds
Food: Worms, shellfish, insects, tadpoles, and small fish

This odd-looking mammal lives on land. But it catches food in the water. The platypus uses its bill to find food on the muddy river bottom. It holds food in its cheek pouches until it returns to the surface.

A mother platypus lays one to three eggs in an underground nest called a burrow. In about ten days, the babies are born blind and without any hair. The mother platypus holds them to her belly as they lick the fur around her milk glands. In four months the babies will learn to swim.

Polar Bear

Classification: Mammal
Home: Arctic regions
Adult Size: 7–11 feet long;
500–1500 pounds
Food: Seals, fish, birds, and berries

Polar bears are well-adapted to life in the icy Arctic regions. A thick layer of fat keeps polar bears warm. White fur hides them as they hunt. Polar bears are very good swimmers. They paddle with their webbed front paws. They steer with their hind legs.

A polar bear mother makes a den in a snowdrift. Her cubs are born there and grow quickly on her milk. A mother protects her cubs from hungry male bears.

Porcupine

Classification: Mammal
Home: Found almost worldwide
Adult Size: About 3 feet long; 15–60 pounds
Food: Fruit, twigs, and bark

A porcupine has more than 30,000 sharp quills on its body. If there is danger, the porcupine swings its tail like a club for protection. It cannot shoot its quills, but they can easily come loose if an enemy gets close enough to be stuck by them. Beneath the quills, thick fur keeps the porcupine warm.

Baby porcupines are born with soft quills that stiffen in a few hours. They live with their mothers for about a year. Then they go off to live on their own.

Puma

Classification: Mammal
Home: North, Central, and South America
Adult Size: 5–7 feet long; 75–200 pounds
Food: Deer and other mammals

This sleek hunter is also called a cougar or mountain lion. The puma is very strong. It can leap as high as 15 feet! Its favorite food is deer, but it preys on many different animals.

A mother puma gives birth in a rocky cave. She will have one to six cubs in a litter. The cubs have rows of black spots that disappear when they get older.

45

Polar Animals

Emperor Penguin

Killer Whale

Walrus

Leopard Seal

Ringed Seal

Great Skua

Arctic Tern

Polar Bear

Musk Ox

Arctic Hare

Arctic Fox

Ptarmigan

47

Q

Quail

Classification: Bird
Home: Every continent except Antarctica
Adult Size: 8–11 inches long; 6¾–7½ ounces
Food: Seeds and insects

Game birds like quails are hunted by many animals, including people. Some quails have colors that make them hard to find. Others have strong legs and can run away from danger. Quails travel in groups called coveys for safety.

Quails build nests among plants on the ground. Then they cover the nests with grass to protect the eggs. A mother quail lays twelve or more eggs at a time. Sometimes the father helps to keep the eggs warm.

Quetzal

Classification: Bird
Home: Mountain forests of Mexico and Central America
Adult Size: Male: over 4 feet long, including tail feathers; 1½–2 pounds
Food: Fruit and insects

Male quetzals have red bodies and green tail feathers that are three feet long. These beautiful birds were worshipped by ancient Aztec and Maya peoples. Quetzals spend most of their time perching quietly on branches.

Quetzals make their nests in tall, dead trees. Mother quetzals lay two eggs once or twice a year. Fathers help to keep the eggs warm until they hatch in about 17 days.

R

Rabbit

Classification: Mammal
Home: Found on all continents except Antarctica
Adult Size: 8–20 inches long; 2–8 pounds
Food: Grasses, flowers, leaves, and crops

Rabbits can hop very fast. They need to be able to move quickly because many, many animals eat rabbits. Rabbits have good hearing and a keen sense of smell. They live in underground burrows called warrens.

Rabbits have many babies. A mother rabbit can have four litters a year. She builds a warm nest snugly lined with some of her own fur. The hairless babies are called kittens or kits. Rabbit kits go off on their own in a few months.

Raccoon

Classification: Mammal
Home: North, Central, and South America
Adult Size: 2–3½ feet long; 8–20 pounds
Food: Frogs, fish, crabs, insects, eggs, rodents, fruit, and nuts

Raccoons are clever animals that make their homes in many different places. Raccoons can use their paws to open doors and trash cans, and even to take lids off jars!

A mother raccoon makes a den in a hollow tree. In the spring, she has one to seven tiny babies. Raccoon kits are very playful. In a year, the kits are old enough to leave their mother.

Reindeer

Classification: Mammal
Home: Northern Europe, Asia, North America
Adult Size: 3–4 feet tall; 250–400 pounds
Food: Grasses and plants in summer; moss and lichen in winter

Both male and female reindeer have antlers. Reindeer have been tamed by people who live near the Arctic. The reindeer carry heavy loads across the snow. People in northern Scandinavia often drink reindeer milk.

Wild reindeer travel in big herds to protect themselves. A mother reindeer has one or two calves. One hour after birth, the calves are able to stand. They quickly learn to run and keep up with the rest of the herd.

Rhinoceros

Classification: Mammal
Home: Africa and Asia
Adult Size: 9–14 feet long; 1 to more than 3 tons
Food: Rough grasses and plants

A rhinoceros has one or two horns on its snout. If a horn breaks off, a new one grows. A big rhino looks clumsy and slow, but if it is angry it can run at a speed of 30 miles per hour!

Rhinos usually have one baby every four years. A baby rhino starts growing a horn right away.

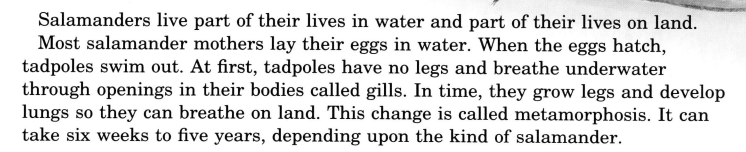

S

Salamander

Classification: Amphibian
Home: All continents except Australia and Antarctica; most common in Asia, Europe, and North America
Adult Size: 2 inches to 5 feet long; 1/10 of an ounce to 30 pounds, depending on the species
Food: Worms, insects, spiders, and slugs

Salamanders live part of their lives in water and part of their lives on land. Most salamander mothers lay their eggs in water. When the eggs hatch, tadpoles swim out. At first, tadpoles have no legs and breathe underwater through openings in their bodies called gills. In time, they grow legs and develop lungs so they can breathe on land. This change is called metamorphosis. It can take six weeks to five years, depending upon the kind of salamander.

Seal

Classification: Mammal
Home: Oceans, lakes, and rivers all over the world, concentrated in colder regions
Adult Size: 4–20 feet long; 200–8,000 pounds
Food: Fish, octopuses, penguins, sea urchins, shellfish, and squid

Seals are mammals. They must breathe air, but some seals can stay underwater for as long as 30 minutes!

In spring, many seal mothers gather on land to give birth at a breeding ground. Each mother usually has one pup at a time. A mother seal knows which baby is hers by its smell and its cry. She nurses her pup for about four months and teaches it how to swim and catch fish.

51

Shark

Classification: Fish
Home: All oceans, some rivers, and freshwater
lakes in warm regions
Adult Size: 5 inches to 50 feet long;
1 ounce to 40,000 pounds
Food: Crabs, dolphins, eels, fish, sea turtles, seals,
stingrays, octopuses, and other sharks

There are many types of shark. Some have four rows of teeth! Sharks use their teeth to grab prey and tear food. When an old tooth falls out, a new one replaces it.

Most sharks give birth to live babies. They are born knowing how to swim. Sharks are born with teeth and can defend themselves right away. Their mothers do not need to take care of them.

Sheep

Classification: Mammal
Home: Domestic sheep: raised in all parts of the world, especially
Europe, New Zealand, Australia, and North and South
America **Wild sheep:** mountainous regions of Asia and
North America
Adult Size: 3–4 feet long; 100–350 pounds
Food: Grass, leaves, plants, vegetables, grain (winter only), and hay

Almost all of the world's wool comes from the fleece of sheep. Sheep shearers remove the sheep's fleece in late spring. The best wool is called lamb's wool. It comes from sheep that are less than one year old.

Lambs are usually born in spring. Sheep have one or two babies at a time. After about ten days, they begin to play with other lambs in the flock. When they are six months old, the sheep are old enough to start families of their own.

Skunk

Classification: Mammal
Home: United States, Canada, Mexico, South and Central America
Adult Size: 12–18 inches long (body only); 3–10 pounds
Food: Berries, corn, seeds, flowers, leaves, fish, frogs, mice, insects, and snakes

When skunks are frightened, they spray a bad-smelling liquid. It can go as far as ten feet. Many other animals leave skunks alone because of their awful smell.

Skunk mothers usually have two to six babies in a litter. Skunk babies are often born in May. Their mothers teach them how to find food. Skunks use their paws to dig or to turn over stones and small logs to find seeds, leaves, and berries.

Snake

Classification: Reptile
Home: Throughout the world, mostly in warmer regions
Adult Size: 10 inches to more than 30 feet long; $\frac{1}{10}$ of an ounce to more than 300 pounds
Food: Birds, eggs, fish, frogs, grasshoppers, mice, rats, rabbits, worms, and other snakes

Snakes swallow their food whole. After a snake swallows an animal, you can see a big bulge in its body. It can go without food for a few weeks after such a big meal.

Some snakes give birth to live young. Others lay eggs. Mothers lay eggs in a warm place—under leaves, rocks, or logs. Many snake mothers leave their eggs as soon as they are laid. Baby snakes can take care of themselves right after they are hatched or born.

Spider

Classification: Arachnid
Home: Throughout the world, except Antarctica
Adult Size: 1/25 of an inch to 3 inches long (body only); 1/1000 of an ounce to 3 ounces
Food: Most small insects, including bees, beetles, flies, grasshoppers, mosquitoes, and other spiders

A spider is not an insect. Insects have six legs, and most of them can fly. Spiders have eight legs and no wings. All spiders eat insects.

Spider mothers lay anywhere from two to one thousand eggs. A newly hatched spider spins a thread of silk called a dragline. It climbs up the dragline to a high place. The air pulls new threads from the spiderling's spinnerets. When the wind blows, the threads float up like balloons, and carry the baby spider far away to a new home.

Squirrel

Classification: Mammal
Home: Throughout the world except Australia, New Zealand, Madagascar, southern South America, and polar regions
Adult Size: 6–30 inches long, including tail; 1/2 ounce to almost 20 pounds
Food: Berries, corn, fruits, vegetables, nuts, and seeds

Tree squirrels have long bushy tails and climb trees. Ground squirrels have short tails and hardly ever climb trees. Woodchucks, chipmunks, and marmots are all ground squirrels.

Tree squirrel mothers usually have two to six babies in one litter. Ground squirrels may have more. Newborn squirrels have no fur. Their eyes are closed. In about a month, their eyes open. Their mothers nurse them until they are about five to eight weeks old. By then, they have all their fur and can begin to find their own food.

Tiger

Classification: Mammal
Home: India, China, Siberia, and Indonesia
Adult Size: 8–11 feet long; 300–500 pounds
Food: Antelope, deer, young elephants,
   wild cattle, and wild pigs

T

Tigers live and hunt alone. They pounce on animals and kill them with their claws and teeth. They can leap 30 feet in a single bound!

Tiger cubs can be born at any time of the year. Tiger mothers usually have three or four cubs in a litter. Cubs practice hunting by chasing one another. They begin to catch their own food when they are one and a half years old.

Tropical Animals

Macaw

Tree Boa

Howler Monkey

Yellow-headed
Parrot

Skeleton Butterfly

Jaguar

Green Amazon Parrot

Orangutan

Squirrel
Monkey

Toucan

Morpho
Butterfly

Blue-tailed
Gecko

Anaconda

Red-eyed
Tree Frog

57

Turkey

Classification: Bird
Home: North and Central America
Adult Size: 4 feet long; 9–16 pounds
Food: Acorns, berries, insects, and seeds

Wild turkeys eat both plants and insects during the daytime. At night, they rest in tree branches.

Turkey mothers build nests on the ground. They lay about ten eggs at a time. The chicks hatch in May or June. Soon after they break out of their shells, turkey chicks follow their mothers to look for food, even though they can find their own food right away. At six months of age, young turkeys are almost fully grown.

Turtle

Classification: Reptile
Home: Oceans, seas, rivers, ponds, deserts, forests, and grasslands of the world, except in Arctic and sub-Arctic regions
Adult Size: 4 inches to 8 feet long; 5 ounces to 1,500 pounds
Food: **Sea turtles:** seaweed, snails, tadpoles, and jellyfish
Land turtles: berries, earthworms, leafy plants, and slugs

Turtles cannot live without their shells. When a turtle is in trouble, it pulls its head, legs, and tail into its shell. This shell protects the slow-moving animal from danger.

Once or twice a year, a turtle mother digs a pit in the mud or sand where she lays up to 200 eggs. Then she leaves. The warmth of the sun will hatch the eggs. The baby turtles dig their way out of the nest. Sea turtles go down to the sea. Baby land turtles move along the sand and away from the pit. The baby turtles must protect themselves and catch food on their own.

U

Urchin

Classification: Echinoderm
Home: Oceans throughout the world
Adult Size: 2–10 inches in diameter
Food: Small sea plants

Urchins are sea animals. They look and feel like pincushions. They have round shells covered with spines. The spines protect sea urchins from their enemies. Sea urchins move on tiny tube-like feet. Sea urchins eat by scraping up plants from the sea bottom with their teeth.

Female urchins lay many, many tiny eggs that float in the water.

V

Vulture

Classification: Bird
Home: Every continent except Australia and Antarctica
Adult Size: 24–56 inches (wingspan up to 10 feet);
2–30 pounds
Food: Dead animals, birds' eggs, and fruit

Vultures don't have to kill other animals for their meals. They feed on animals that are already dead.

Vulture mothers usually lay one to three eggs at a time. Parents take turns sitting on the eggs to keep them warm until they hatch. Vulture chicks stay in their nests for eight to ten weeks. Their parents cough up soft food for the chicks to eat. Vultures leave their nests when they are fully grown and able to fly.

Walrus

Classification: Mammal
Home: Arctic waters
Adult Size: 10–12 feet long;
             1,000–3,500 pounds
Food: Clams, mussels, and sea worms

Adult walruses have ivory tusks that can be more than three feet long! Their chubby bodies are covered in thick blubber. The blubber can be six inches thick in places. It helps protect them from the cold Arctic waters.

Walrus calves are born on ice floes, often in the month of May. A walrus mother teaches her calf to swim. She takes the baby into the water on her back. A baby walrus drinks its mother's milk for almost two years. By then, it will be able to take care of itself, using its tusks to dig for food on the ocean floor.

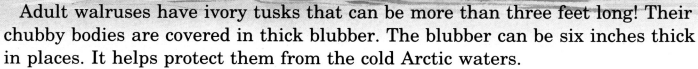

Whale

Classification: Mammal
Home: All oceans
Adult Size: 20–110 feet long; 4½–150 tons
Food: Tiny sea plants and animals, fish, seals, sea lions, and squid

Whales cannot breathe underwater as fish can. Whales are mammals. They must go up to the surface for air. Whales breathe through blowholes at the top of their heads.

Whale mothers usually give birth to one baby at a time. A newborn whale can swim. But its mother must push it up to the surface for air. During its first year, the baby whale stays close to its mother. The mother teaches her baby how to dive, how to hold its breath under water, and how to find food.

Wombat

Classification: Mammal
Home: Australia and Tasmania
Adult Size: 3–4 feet long; 30–80 pounds
Food: Grass, plants, roots, and shrubs

Wombats dig burrows that are sometimes more than 100 feet long! The burrows protect the wombats against heat and cold. Wombats stay in their burrows during the day and go out at night to nibble on grass and shrubs.

Wombats, like kangaroos, are marsupials. A newborn wombat is the size of a small bean! It stays in its mother's pouch and drinks her milk for about six months. When it grows teeth, it can begin to eat grass. Even when it can live out of the pouch, the wombat stays close to its mother for about a year.

X

Xanthid crabs use their claws to defend themselves and to tear up their food.

Crab mothers lay hundreds of eggs in deep water. A baby crab changes its shell many times. The shell cannot stretch while the crab grows. A young crab splits its shell and wriggles out of it. A new shell is growing underneath. When it is three years old, a crab reaches its adult size.

Xanthid Crab

Classification: Crustacean
Home: North America, Atlantic and Pacific coasts
Adult Size: 1–4 inches; 1 ounce to one pound
Food: Barnacles, mussels, and small oysters

Y

Yak

Classification: Mammal
Home: Asia, highlands of Tibet
Adult Size: 6 feet high at the
         shoulder; 1,100–
         1,200 pounds
Food: Grass, shrubs, and lichens

Yaks have thick, shaggy coats of fur. Their fur keeps them warm in the freezing cold of the mountains where they live. Yaks like to eat in the morning and rest in the afternoon.

Mother yaks usually give birth to one baby at a time. A baby yak can walk and follow its mother within a few hours after it is born. A baby yak stays close to its mother until it is one and a half years old. Then, it is ready to have a family of its own.

Z

Zebra

Classification: Mammal
Home: Africa, from Ethiopia to South Africa
Adult Size: 4–5 feet high at the shoulder; 650–950 pounds
Food: Grass and plants

Zebras look like ponies with stripes. Each zebra has its own pattern of stripes. Zebras live in herds that are divided into smaller groups, each led by a stallion.

Mother zebras usually give birth to one baby, or foal, at a time. When the zebra foal is being born, the father stands nearby to protect the mother. The baby lives on its mother's milk for a few days. Then it begins nibbling on grass. Young zebras live close to their mothers for about one year. Then they leave to join another group in the herd.

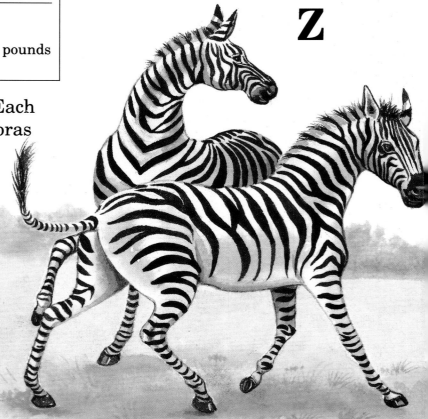

Animal Families

Scientists have found more than one million kinds of animals in the world today. Scientists use many different ways to sort animals into groups or categories. Here are the animal classifications used in *My First Book of Animals From A to Z*.

Amphibians
Amphibians are cold-blooded animals. That means their body temperatures change depending on how cold or hot their environments are. They all have backbones. When they are very young, they live in water. When they are fully grown, they live on land near water. Frogs, newts, and toads are all amphibians.

Arachnids
Arachnids have no backbones. Unlike insects, their bodies are divided into two parts. Arachnids have eight legs and no antennae. Spiders are arachnids.

Birds
Birds are warm-blooded animals, which means their body temperatures stay the same regardless of the temperature in their environments. They all have two wings, two legs, a backbone, a bill, and feathers. Most, but not all, birds can fly.

Crustaceans
Crustaceans are animals with jointed bodies and hard shells. When a crustacean is growing, it sheds its shell and grows a new one. Crustaceans live mostly in water. Crabs and lobsters are crustaceans.

Echinoderms
Echinoderms are sea animals. All echinoderms have body parts that are arranged around the center of the animal. Starfish, urchins, and sand dollars are echinoderms.

Fish
Fish are cold-blooded animals that live in water. They have backbones and breathe through gills. Most fish have fins and scales.

Insects
Insects are small animals. Their bodies are divided into three parts—the head, the thorax, and the abdomen. Insects have six legs and, usually, two pairs of wings. Wasps and flies are insects.

Mammals
Mammals are warm-blooded animals that are developed within the mother. Newborn mammals drink milk from their mothers. Most mammals are covered with a layer of fur. Mice and humans are mammals.

Mollusks
Mollusks have no backbones. Their soft bodies are protected by hard shells. Mollusks live in water. Clams and snails are members of the mollusk family.

Reptiles
Reptiles are cold-blooded. They have backbones and dry skin. Most reptiles hatch from eggs. Snakes and lizards are members of the reptile family.

INDEX

All entries in italics are illustrations only.